GOT SCOOP?

TIPS ON WORKING AND LANDING A JOB AS A CELEBRITY REPORTER

TANISHA WILLIAMS

Printed in the United States of America

In order to protect the identity of certain individuals, some of the defining attributes such as names, physical characteristics, and locations have been changed.

For information, please visit:

www.gotscoop.com

Cover art and design by: UmyRaff

ISBN: 9798375989235

First Edition

February 2019

ACKNOWLEDGEMENTS

Thank you to Pat Means, Turning Point Magazine for giving me a chance, Sidney Miller, Publisher of BRE Magazine for shining a light on me, Tony Coughlan, Los Angeles Bureau Chief and Managing Editor of Inside Edition for igniting my curiosity, and Martha Flores, US Weekly for showing me the way to a great story.

To those who want it badly enough.

TABLE OF CONTENTS

FOREWARD

"Luck is what happens when preparation meets opportunity."
Seneca Roman

Although I graduated from one of the nation's top-ranked schools for journalism - I discovered early on that I still had so much to learn when it came to landing a job in the entertainment business. People think it's easy to get into this industry, and in some ways, it can be, and in some ways, it may not be. Many people aren't willing to do the work it takes to get in the door. In my early twenties, I remember watching all of the journalism television shows standing in the grocery store for hours, and looking at magazines at the end. I couldn't get enough of it and would dream of someday working at a magazine. Years later when I moved to California, I set my eyes on doing just that; I looked up all the companies I could think of, tried to find a contact for anyone I could, and wrote to them about writing for free or interning.

Other than writing a few articles for my college school newspaper, I didn't have tons of experience, but I knew if I was given the opportunity, I would shine. The first magazine job I landed was as an Executive Assistant for the publisher of a small business magazine called "Turning Point." It was a family-owned publication, but since it was so small, I was able to insert myself into all sides of the business and learn how the publication was put together. Eventually, I started asking if I could write and do interviews, and eventually, I was given the opportunity. This only fed my desire so much more that, I began looking to write and offer my services any chance I got.

I thought about other skills I had and began writing to the different entertainment companies for any positions that fit those skills just so I could get in the door. Eventually, the news magazine "Inside Edition," called and hired me as a transcriber. I worked tirelessly to transcribe all the interviews during the night shift, and when I found out they were hiring an assignment editor, I jumped at the chance. This is an example of being in the right place at the right time; I was offered the job and left "Turning Point" for "Inside Edition." I worked for over three years on the assignment desk, interviewing potential guests, looking for story leads, pitching stories, working with posts, booking feeds, and more. Over the years, I would continue to seek out new opportunities. So, when a friend told me that E! Entertainment was seeking to hire a News Editor for the Daily 10 show, I jumped at the chance.

I remember the first day at E! and how excited I was to see all of the familiar faces I saw across my television screen in my youth. It felt like home, and I was finally where I needed to be. The show was busy and always had exciting guests. The responsibilities were endless. Honestly, since writing at "Turning Point," I still had that desire to write. So, I started submitting my resume and landed a part-time reporter position with the infamous "US Weekly," magazine. As I moonlighted at night doing club reporting and back-reporting during the weekends, the editors at "US Weekly" appreciated my hard work. My work on a story about a reality tv star who endured tragedy after her sister's boyfriend killed her family members got their attention. I was tasked with reaching out to friends and family members, and I made it my duty to be compassionate to them, and it made them want to open up to me much more. Tragedies like this are always a sensitive topic, so use your instincts to proceed. This is especially true when it comes to announcing a death to a loved one; many times, they aren't the first to know, and it can be quite jarring. The next thing I knew, I was asked to come into the US Weekly offices and meet with the News Director. I was offered a reporter position, and the next 6 years would be the craziest ride ever through award seasons, interviews, celebrity scandals, and more. I definitely have enough stories to share to write a series, but that's not what this is about. It's about how badly you want it. I wanted it so bad that I never stopped pursuing it until I got there.

This is the story that landed me at US Weekly.

Here's a clue.

I was very specific about the outreach I did; I sharpened my interviewing skills by offering to write for free, and I worked hard to build relationships and my portfolio of work. Also, remember that your portfolio reflects your brand as a reporter, so utilize it to position yourself as an authority by providing clips, writing samples, and your resume to make a deeper impression. If you don't have anything at this time, get started. Work for the school newspaper, create your own content and submit it, or use your summers to intern. Don't be afraid to ask for the opportunity, and when you get it, kill it!

It's easy to continue asking for a job, a favor, or a referral from others, but you want to also show how you can provide value. I knew I enjoyed writing and interviewing and offered that whenever I could. Maybe you prefer to be on-camera, in the newsroom, or out in the field scouring stories. Tap into that and use it to your advantage early on in your career. That will set you apart from someone else who's new in the industry and constantly looking to be taught something. Of course, you are going to learn the other segments of the business as you work in the environment, but providing value is how you level up.

As an entertainment reporter, you can end up covering breaking news stories, attending red carpets, investigating leads, writing, and much more. Other than the valuable world experience you gain, the rewards can be endless.

That's why I wrote **"Got Scoop? Trade Tips of Working and Landing a Job as a Celebrity Reporter,"** to help you unlock a career and thrive in the entertainment industry. So, get comfortable because I'm going to give you the skinny on what you should know as you step into this dynamic and ever-evolving world of celebrity journalism.

CHAPTER 1

INSIDE THE NEWSROOM

8 Traits of a Great Reporter

During my time working at several entertainment companies, one of the first lessons I learned was the importance of being invested in the story. While most believe that it's simply about being in the right place at the right time, the life blood of your groundbreaking story is in the leads you generate and the interviews you conduct.

So, how can you reach your goal of becoming a great reporter?

First, you need to understand your role and responsibilities. On the most basic level, your job is to research and convert information into various types of mass media. This means that your content is widely distributed to and reached by large audiences. Secondly, reporting is all about the hunt for information including researching tips from sources, spending time in the field to determine what is newsworthy, getting first-hand information from actual interviews, and back-reporting. We will discuss this in more detail later in the book.

All this falls into what's known in the journalism world as "cultivating your beat or your story" (aka covering a specific topic, area, person, or event). As a celebrity reporter, you will spend most of your time in the field with boots on the ground knocking on doors, interviewing people, and gathering public records (Think TMZ). As you perfect your craft, you may even get assigned a story to work on or a particular beat. One of my first beats as an entertainment reporter for US Weekly magazine was covering a famous pop star. I was pretty much thrown into the process of covering this pop singer day and night. I sat with the paparazzi and built relationships, learned my subject's whereabouts, and how they moved. I was able to uncover inside information and build the trust of peers around the pop star to secure a few tidbits to round my stories out every now and then. There were some ups and downs, but I learned the following traits you should have on your way to becoming a great reporter.

01. INSATIABLE CURIOSITY:

When I was working at Inside Edition as the assignment editor on the news desk, I remember feeling overwhelmed at the idea of having to find captivating stories to assign to the reporters. Then one day, as I was flippantly scanning the news wires for interesting stories, the Bureau Chief saw the empty look on my face, turned to me then, glanced at the TV, and asked me why the story playing in the background had the potential to make a great lead.

At the time, I wasn't sure, and with a slight look of annoyance on his face, he fixed his gaze on me and said,

"Tanisha, you must be curious. You must read stories and find the nugget that's missing. What isn't being said in this story? Who hasn't been interviewed? Is there a story within this story?"

TONY COGHLAN
LA BUREAU CHIEF & MANAGING EDITOR - INSIDE EDITION

If my memory serves me correctly, the story was about a mother whose child got stuck in a cage at a zoo. He promptly followed up with: What happened with the caretaker of the animal? Who is the woman that is comforting the mom? What's her story? Has this ever happened at this zoo before, or is this a problem for others, too?

Check out the most recent update of this story by Inside Edition:

Just from that instance alone, he pointed out four stories, and from that moment on, I applied his advice whenever I landed a story and when I covered one. If you implement this thought process, you will develop an insatiable curiosity. It's as simple as scrolling through social media, reading blogs and magazines to see beyond the story that's presented and into the potential of what it could be. Remember, there's always more to a story than just the headline. Get curious.

02. PAY ATTENTION TO DETAIL:

During my time at E!, Part of my job was to book and organize a variety of shoots for the producers. This was an awesome gig, but very stressful, and you had to pay attention to detail at all times. I learned this lesson the hard way during my time at E! I was rushing to book an on-air shoot from an entirely different state, setting up a photo shoot at the last minute, and a few other items I had to meet the deadline. Unfortunately, it turned out that I booked a shoot for the wrong day on this occasion. The entire day spiraled out of control, and not only was it a disaster, but I had to juggle the same projects and work hard to correct the situation. This mistake impacted everyone down, from the producers, stylists, photographers, make-up artists, creative directors, and everyone in between. Needless to say, I was embarrassed, but I learned one important lesson: Slow down and make sure to review necessary details the day before while ensuring everyone is on the same page. There was nothing you could get me to stray from the details that I needed to know for the next day from that point on. We are all human, so we will make mistakes. However, what's important in these situations is how you respond when they happen. While it does take humility and courage to own your mistakes, making the necessary adjustments so that they don't happen again will help you to resolve the situation more quickly and earn the respect of your supervisors and colleagues

03. BUILD TRUST:

As a reporter, you are going to run in some of the most powerful and influential circles of people. This means that there are higher standards of excellence regarding how you show up every day. To build trust and rapport with those with whom you come into contact, you need to stay abreast of all that's happening industry-wide. What does this mean exactly? It means that your beat must become your specialization or expertise. This is how you build relationships and familiarity. You want to know who the major and minor players are, the story surrounding your beat, and what the editors are looking for. When they see that you are taking the initiative, that builds trust on the inside. To achieve this, start gathering up everything you can about your beat, including exclusive interviews, popular shows, and trending topics or news items as much as possible. The more you do this, the more intuitive it will become.

---

04. THE X-FACTOR:

During my time in the newsroom, I became somewhat of a super detective. It turns out that my naturally extroverted personality was an asset when it came to gathering information, and my bosses took notice. It's the same for you. In the entertainment industry, you have to figure out what's going to set you apart from the rest of the reporters. What's something you can do really well? Do you already have a rolodex of celebrity pals? Do you love to locate news stories through sources? What about building contacts by offering exposure to them? Perhaps your charisma and ability to build long-lasting relationships with others are through the roof. You want to hone in on your X-Factor, or your unique area of extraordinary ability? Think it through. We all have an X-Factor; however, if you still have a hard time finding it, don't be afraid to zero in on something you enjoy doing and create it.

05. TAKE THE INITIATIVE:

Reporters in the celebrity entertainment have to possess a level of drive that's higher than that of a typical news reporter because the competition is fierce, and the pressure is always on. Don't be afraid to speak up when you have something to say or ask. The best forum for these opportunities is either at a press junket for an awards show or even if your outlet lands a one-on-one interview. Use your time wisely, ask intelligent, responsible questions, and you'll be surprised by the response. While reporters have to toe the line between being objectively focused and fiercely tenacious, knowing when to speak up and ask questions will help you in your career. During my earlier days at E!, in those high-pressure moments, I thought it better to stick to the script. However, ultimately, I could have passed on landing an incredible story.

06. THINK OUTSIDE THE BOX:

When searching for a story, you want to exhaust all of your resources. It's easy to piggyback on a story that is already out there, but what happens when you stumble upon your own story? As I mentioned earlier, one assignment can always lead you to another. Now, if you really want to stand out to your editors, the key is to take the initiative to get the story without having your hand held every step of the way. For example, one time, I was doing a report on a well-respected celebrity, and I had to do what's known in the industry as back reporting to get the story.[1] When this individual left the establishment, I came in to ask the staff what they observed, and based on their eyewitness accounts, I was able to develop a story that my readers cared about. However, when I first started working at US Magazine, I would sometimes come back to the office empty-handed, and my boss would ask, "You went to the place where x-celebrity was last seen, but what about the neighboring establishments to see if they walked into any of those?" Honestly, at the time, it never crossed my mind to check them. After that meeting, I was able to return to those establishments and uncover all the juicy details I needed for my story that were nowhere to be found on social media. Still to this day, I believe that good reporting does not limit itself to conventional methodology, so if you want the story, go out and get it.

07. A PASSION FOR NEWS:

Did you know that the vast majority of college students enrolled in journalism programs do not read or watch the news? It's true, and this eyebrow-raising phenomenon is easily the most overlooked quality of great reporters. So, how can knowing this help you land your first job as an entertainment reporter? First, most newbie reporter will express their passion for social media, celebrities, and entertainment but not their knowledge of the news, which means that you now have the distinct advantage that if you stay connected to current and unfolding events, you will see a whole world open up to you for the taking. Eventually, this could lead to you being asked to be an expert and provide commentary on a specialty that you have honed. People will take notice.

08. INTEGRITY:

Last but not least, I want you to understand that in journalism, there exists only one universal truth - Integrity above all. In other words, there is no such thing as having a "little bit of integrity" or having it "some of the time". As a reporter, you either have it, or you don't, and if your desire is to become a great reporter, you must have the highest standards when it comes to accountability, truth, and ethics. Why? Well, you could find yourself in some seriously hot water with defamation lawsuits, copyright violations, or privacy infringement if you didn't. The key is to remember that trust that you have done your due diligence. Remember, people will come to you if your stories have not been vetted properly, which could affect your career and how others in the industry view you.

---

1   *Back reporting is when a reporter goes to an establishment (i.e., restaurant, store, gym, etc.) that a celebrity has already frequented to ask the witnesses what they observed.*

SHINING IN PITCH MEETINGS

Before you see people shining in pitch meetings, you usually see them shrink. A pitch meeting can be one of the most gruesome moments of your day if you're not prepared.

A pitch meeting is where you present your story ideas to your editor in front of the entire team to see what makes the final call about its newsworthiness and whether they should be covered for publication. The news cycle is non-stop, but, for the most part, it recycles every Tuesday. So, every 7 days, you start over with new news, updates, breaking news, and creating news.

Pitch meetings are nerve-racking. I remember a colleague of mine had panic attacks every Tuesday morning, but once you begin to apply yourself, it gets easier. Here are my 5 tips when pitching:

01. COME PREPARED

When I first started working for US Magazine, the pitch meetings caused me the most anxiety because I wasn't sure how to prepare. As a result, my first few story pitches were received with an awkward silence. That's obviously not what you want, so to deliver a successful pitch, you should be able to research the stories your outlet is currently working on and how you can expand the story, source new stories, and book upcoming stories that are relevant to your outlet. When you are deciding this, you want to ask yourself:

- Is the story relevant? Is it timely? Is it trending? Is it factual?
- What's more important to the readers?
- What type of piece is this? Where does it fit in our breakdown?
- Does the story have a unique angle or twist?
- Do you have the relevant sources to develop this story?

02. TIME IS OF THE ESSENCE:

Being prepared when you go into the room is everything, but how you share the information is another. You don't have much time to impress and gain the room's interest, so remember, when you make your shot, you have to be on point. Be a little aggressive about your story and have the facts laid.

03. KNOW YOUR STORY ANGLE.

To find your angle, tune in to the conversations of those around you and regularly check online for trending topics before the day of the pitch meeting. Remember, a great reporter is always looking, observing, and scanning for the unusual, the ironic, and the unique. I once had to do a story about a celebrity losing baby weight with their trainer and was working on trying to figure out how she was feeling and her emotional and mental state as a new mom. So, I set up a meeting with the trainer, and out of that, I got the information I needed, found out the regimen the trainer used, and did a story on him and his celebrity fitness regimen for celebs losing baby weight. So, that's two stories in one. Take the time to brainstorm and remember that there is value even in the smaller items; you just have to uncover them.

04. SEASONAL ANGLES.

Pitches with seasonal ties can add an extra layer of relevance to your story ideas. For example, the new year is a great time for pitches on goals and resolutions while the end of the year is great for holiday-related content. Keep an eye on seasonal trends and find unique ways to tie your pitches to fashionable moments.

05. KEEP A JOURNAL.

New leads can come from anywhere. So, to ensure that you are always prepared, keep a record of your ideas. This will also prevent "pitcher's block where you feel like you're out of fresh takes and insights. What does keeping a journal look like in real time for reporters? Well, as they go through their day, any inkling of a potential story is immediately written down. This allows them to have a secret place where their creativity can flow without judgment or critique, which ensures that they always have pitch ideas to fall back on. Don't forget the go-to topics that you can generate stories on such as How-To or Top 10. These are green items that you can repurpose over and over again.

Here's a story I re-purpose into a HOW TO :
FERGIE'S TRAINER: HOW TO GET A-LIST LEGS

Shining in pitch meetings

DOS AND DON'TS IN THE NEWSROOM

THE NEWSROOM

The newsroom is chaotic and exciting because the news has to be thought of in a hybrid model. For example, most major news publications have to produce both digital and print content to get views, clicks, and readership. This means that the one-trick pony model is long gone, as everything is about getting as many eyeballs in front of your content as quickly as possible. Additionally, with celebrities and creators doing their own social media lives, reels, tweets, Tik-toks, Instagram posts, podcasts, blogs, YouTube videos, etc., you have to be ready for anything at any moment.

The pressure is so intense at times that you never want to be the person who dropped the ball on a story, particularly if you work for one of the bigger media establishments. However, if you can handle the pressure, you will learn how to build sources and fast-track information. You'll start developing a sense of what's good about a story, so that you can predict fairly well what's going to work and what's not. You'll also develop an instinct beyond the stories and into the photos, events, tweets, and events that will engage your audience because you'll constantly be putting in the work to push out content.

As a reporter, you will be expected to perform a variety of tasks, so to help you fulfill your role, here are my most highly recommended Do's and Don'ts for when you're working in the newsroom.

DO...

Know the publication.

Reporter have to understand not only what their audience wants but also the needs of the publication. To have success in this area, ask other professional writers what they've written about in the past and which stories received the most engagement. Additionally, flip through the magazines and websites to see what stories have been of interest lately and why the audience gravitates towards them. Additionally, talk to your editor regarding the frequency of new story announcements. How often and when do they occur? What are normal weekly deadlines?

DO...

Adhere to the chain of command.

In case this wasn't clear before, major publications have a chain of command that starts with the publisher at the top, then the editors, and then you, the reporter. What this means is that your direct report is to your editor. So, as you navigate the newsroom, utilize the chain of command when you have questions involving sources, ethics, and credibility rather than broadcasting them at pitch meetings. Additionally, as you build relationships with others, remember that vibration is king. As a new reporter, stay focused on building relationships with those who want to see you succeed.

DO...

Observe deadlines.

To harness the positive energy in this industry, you need to become a person of your word. Meeting your deadlines in this business is everything. Showing up on time is everything. Responding to inquiries in a timely fashion is everything. All of this plays into your brand as a reporter. Also, the news is a 24-hour cycle, so if you don't operate well under pressure or you struggle with meeting deadlines in general, you'll want to do some serious soul-searching as to whether this career is for you.

DO...

Adopt office dress and cultural standards.

As a reporter, you'll want to interweave the office culture with your personal style. Now, while most newsrooms I've worked at have had fairly casual standards regarding dressing and grooming, remember that how you project yourself ultimately speaks to what type of person you are. Personally, I've always made it a point to look my best because I believe that presentation is a huge component of my success in this industry. Also, remember that anything you say (or do) can and will be held against you as someone working in the public eye.

DO...

Capitalize on your mistakes.

Mishaps, misunderstandings, miscommunication, and mistakes will happen, but the key is to learn from them so that they don't repeat themselves. So, as you develop your skills, research moments of celebrity reporter both dominating the industry and falling on their faces so that you can learn not just from your own mistakes but their.

---

as well. Then, once you see what works, you can then make yourself more relatable, knowledgeable, and likeable while allowing your talent and expertise to speak for themselves.

DON'T...

Vanish from the office.

Journalism is really a team sport because, behind every story, there are editors, writers, producers, graphic designers, photographers, and even marketers. As such, your team is counting on you to be there, especially when there's a breaking story. In essence, communication is key. So, if you need to leave to attend to a personal matter, communicate that with your boss and team members. Also, think of others. If you're stepping out to grab a latte, ask others if they'd like you to grab them something on your way out. This shows that you're putting the team first.

DON'T...

Complain about an assignment.

Getting an assignment is a privilege understanding the value of that will help you to succeed because when you are assigned a beat, it means that your bosses trust you and value your work. That's why it's important to stay positive. Will you work long days? Yes. Will you work long nights? Yes. Will you pay your dues? Definitely, but remember that it's not forever. Everyone who continues to show up day in and day out eventually graduates to something bigger and better. For example, after covering celebrity beats for a number of years, I eventually was able to cover award shows, which let me tell you, is the crème de la crème of celebrity journalism.

DON'T...

Gossip about stories you're working on.

Consider Hollywood a small town and the media as the local hangout where everyone knows everybody's business. As such, you'll want to be selective about whom you confide in. Information spreads like wildfire in this industry, and with journalism being so competitive, you don't want people to steal your scoop simply because you gave them too much information. Remember that people are always racing to get to the punch first, so play your cards close to the chest.

CHAPTER 2

WRITING THE ARTICLE

The Role of the Reporter

Your role as a celebrity reporter is to uncover the news within the entertainment industry. Good reporting, though, is a process. It requires extensive amounts of research, a keen eye for detail, and a passion for the careers and lives of modern-day icons. To gather information for your reports, let's look at four of the most effective techniques and reporting styles.

BACK-REPORTING

Back-reporting may be considered a thing of the past with the advent of social media; however, it's still a cool trick to have it in your bag. This technique is all about getting the scoop on your subject from others' observations or first hand accounts. You gather this information, and this can become a story. What were they eating? How was the conversation? Was anyone sad? Did they seem like they were getting married? Is this a new relationship blossoming? The angles depending on what's happening and what story could develop can go on and on. For example, one of my reports revolved around a famous celebrity couple who had been spotted at a high-end car dealership. The couple was thinking about purchasing an expensive SUV, and based on some tactical information from sources, we gathered that they were having a baby and wanted a more utilitarian, luxury-style vehicle.

Early in my career, I also had to cover a high-profile celebrity whose relationships with family members were hot news. This meant that every chance I got, I was analyzing their body language, studying their family history, and learning the ins and outs of the family dynamic. With regards to back-reporting, I followed up with everyone they spoke to at stores, restaurants, and cafes, which was how I landed a few stories in the Hot Topics section of *US Weekly*. Back-reporting has served me well over the years, as taking copious notes, analyzing photos, and, most importantly, speaking with eyewitnesses almost always yielded a newsworthy story. How so? In the entertainment industry, content is king and there's no shortage.

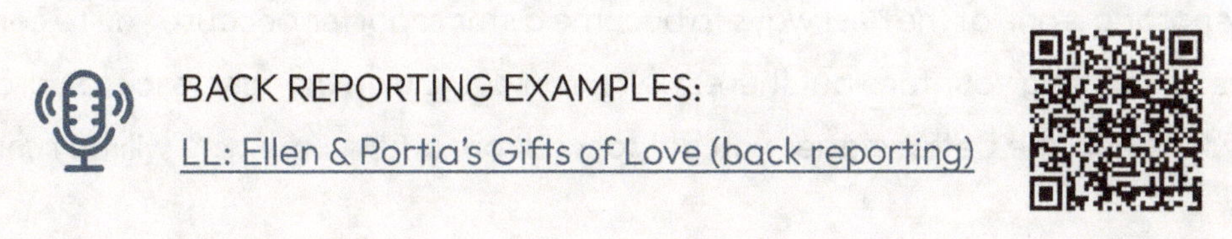

FIELD REPORTING

The second technique is field reporting. This is where your investigative skills come to the forefront because you're either covering a specific story, (possibly a huge break up, marriage, baby news, you name it) or you're in the field where you are on the hunt to uncover a story that has been reported. Maybe there is a new relationship on set, and you are sent to the movie set, or you're trying to find out inside information on when the last season will air. I remember being on the set of a very popular television show that is still on air. I mean, it was so difficult to get on set, but once I was there, I couldn't believe it. I spent hours just hanging around trying to get someone's attention, and suddenly a production coordinator took notice of me, and I pretended like I was a huge fan of the show, and he offered to take me closer. He also began to share some cool behind the scenes stories that were happening. I was officially in. I ended up spending the entire day with him on this set and walked away with some great tidbits. Unfortunately, when you are field reporting, you can't always provide your identity because you're not supposed to be there. I mean, if you want to get kicked out immediately, then do just that. It can be a little stressful at first, but if you don't get the scoop, someone else will.

One time I had to do an entire weekend of field reporting for a famous reality star's wedding. We were booked into the hotel for the wedding party, and the games began. Ironically, we weren't alone, and there were tons of other reporters also booked into the same hotel. That was a wild weekend; however, building trust with the guests of the wedding party didn't take long, and they began to share fun stories about the bride and groom, photos, and the schedule of the festivities. This is a golden ticket for any celebrity reporter. From there, I was able to get half of the information I needed for my story. The other half came from a family source. (Yes, people close to celebrities do share information at times, and this was a source close to the bride and groom, so I hit the jackpot.)

 Would you like to know who's the wedding?
Here's a hint. 

In summary, field reporting is one of the best ways to become a star reporter because you're constantly developing a nose for the news and putting your face out there, which can put you on the fast track towards success. How so? The more stories you break, the better stories you get to work on, and in time, you will be running the newsroom yourself.

It's not all rosy because sometimes you can become conflicted with your job and the fact that you do have to be inconspicuous at times. I remember my first field reporting assignment was covering one of the most notorious pop stars, and I covered her beat for months as she began to unravel publicly. It was really sad seeing her being followed constantly and literally swarmed by the paparazzi wherever she went. It was difficult, but I had to separate my emotions from my job during that time to get through it. I had to report on what was going on and be subjective. So, there are times when you may get more emotionally involved, but you're a professional ,so act like it.

EVENT REPORTING

You would think that this is the easiest reporting, right? Wrong. I mean yes, you get assigned an event, and you hit the red carpet and ask questions and get to go inside and mix and mingle. Sometimes yes, it does happen that way, however, depends on the event. Award shows can be grueling and hours long. Sometimes on the red-carpet other reporters try to steal your position and your scoop, so you have to be on top of it. There are tons of celebrities that may or may not show up, and you most definitely don't want to offend anyone waiting anxiously to interview the people whom the editor wants quotes from, so it's a fine line. Typically, the outlet will have their selected 1000 questions that they prefer you to ask, but the biggest mistake many reporter make is not preparing for these events because they seem so easy. Arrive early so that you can get to the best spot possible. Wear comfortable shoes. You'll thank me. Memorize the two questions that you need to ask, but, most of all, research and make sure you know who the celebrity is, what project they are with and what they look like. You would be amazed how many reporters get this information wrong and end up embarrassing themselves or offending the celebrity. One tip I want to share is to find out a tidbit that no one else may know about them; maybe they went to your alma mater or grew up in the same city. This is a great warm-up introduction and opens the door for your subject to feel comfortable when speaking with you.

EXAMPLE OF EVENT REPORTING:

BET AWARDS 2007

SOURCE REPORTING

Building a network of sources is non-stop. Anyone can be a source. A gardener, doctor, family member, nanny, the local boutique the celebrity shops at, or the postman. This type of reporting can garner a ton of information if you do it right. This also includes experts, eyewitnesses, and other credible individuals to assemble the nuts and bolts of your story.

For example, in the early 2000s, big-name superstars were partiers, and reporters could spot them fairly easily at the hottest clubs and bars. However, most celebrities now party in private settings, which means that in order to get the 411, you are largely dependent on your sources.

TO CULTIVATE YOUR LIST, REMEMBER THESE KEY PRINCIPLES:

Meet people where they are. If you can't access the celebrities themselves, connect with the people who represent and or around them. Offer an opportunity to cover an upcoming project, movie, or even a lesser talent for any type of scoop.

Make friends with the paparazzi. Over the years, relationships between paparazzi and celebrities have been tempestuous at best, but despite this, they are still one of your best sources for lead generation. Times have changed drastically with social media, and everyone is a paparazzi. Don't believe the hype, though; they are still out there. Remember the day when you didn't know how to identify if a paparazzi was around? It's an old-age profession that may be shrinking at the moment, but it's still around. The paparazzi study celebrities like it's a sport. They know what they drive, what their kids look like, their favorite hangouts, and even popular routes that they travel. This means that as a celebrity reporter, the paparazzi are your new best friend. I remember when I started reporting at *US Weekly,* my first beat was to cover a high-profile celebrity who was going through some rocky times, both personally and professionally. This individual was followed night and day from the moment they left their house to the moment they returned, and I was along for the ride. Each day I would wait alongside the paparazzi, and soon, I built a relationship with enough of them that they would call me with updates and news.

Pap source story: My Pap source and details
for Ryan Gosling and Eva Mendes Romance

Your job as a celebrity reporter is to tell the story. This doesn't mean that you break the law or play dirty, though. What it does mean, however, is that, as far as it depends on you, you must work with celebrities with the understanding that this industry can be cut-throat and that public places are fair game for stories, videos, and photographs. Afterall, your livelihood depends on it.

Treat the little people like the big people. It's in your best interest, especially when networking, to treat interns, assistants, and receptionists like GOLD. Most people think they need to connect with the 'bigwigs' to get the inside scoop, but it's quite the opposite. If you focus on cultivating great relationships with the individuals that work behind the scenes (you know, the ones who are always running errands and grabbing coffee for the boss), your chances of generating a lead skyrocket. Why? Think of it this way. These are the individuals that often feel overlooked and undervalued. They're also just as hungry as you are to get their foot in the door, which means that if you treat them with dignity and respect, especially when they probably feel like a nobody, they're likely to stick by you as you both climb your way to the top. Word to the wise, though. Don't ever go into these situations thinking, "What's in it for me?" Focus on their needs without the expectation of getting something in return to create genuine business partnerships that will last a lifetime.

Utilize social media to connect. Repeat after me. *Your network is your net worth. Your network is your net worth. Your network is your net worth.* Social media is the tool of the ages, and as long as you put in the time to cultivate and nurture relationships online, you're going to be able to expedite the process of reporting glory. Yes, it's true that when you finally get a big break, most will say that you were just lucky, but there's nothing lucky about making genuine connections and strategic partnerships with people online. Also, recognize that the most successful people in this industry were not rugged individualists. *But aren't they sharing and promoting their own content?* Of course, they are, but the truly great are always thinking collectively and collaboratively. This means that there are people on social media who want to share their knowledge with you and help you speed up the process, but you have to invest in yourself enough to go find them. Another great way is to connect with a celebrity's fan club captains. They are always keeping their ear to the ground on the celebrity they cover, and often will notice when something is in the works before the media does.

Watch for up-and-coming talent. One specific way that you can build your network of sources and connections is by connecting with up-and-coming talent. For example, let's say you're on TikTok or Instagram, and you notice a gifted singer, or a brilliant artist in your area. Take the time to go up to that individual and introduce yourself in recognition of the fact that they are going to be great. From there, focus on figuring out ways to get these individuals more visibility, which will build your brand as a reporter. By taking the initiative, you will establish yourself as a credible reporter with not only an eye for a story, but as someone who understands the hustle it takes to succeed. Afterall, it's not always the most talented or the most educated who make it in this industry. It's the people who can command attention.

Always be a reporter. If you're just starting out in your journalism career, I've got some good news for you: *The average person is not going through their day thinking about how they can turn life events into content for a news network.* However, as an aspiring celebrity reporter, you can gain a competitive edge by understanding that everyone has a story to tell. Whether it's a secret romantic rendezvous, a celebrity scandal, or a comeback story, start scouring the internet for information that you can compile into a potential blog, headline, caption, or even hashtag. As you go through each day, ask yourself, "What can I learn from this experience?", "How does this story connect with current trends?", and "How do these facts relate with one another?" Even when you want to let your guard down, you have to remember the job you are there to do.

While covering a beat for a woman who was an ordinary citizen, the fact that she was having a brood of children changed her life forever. She was being hounded by the paparazzi every day. I became so exhausted over it. I mean, she couldn't come home without seeing 10 cars outside her house, and she was quite understandably frustrated and horrified most days. Over the weeks I had to be there, I made sure to speak and do my job, but I respected her boundaries. So, she started to feel comfortable around me. I ensured I was also kind when I spoke with her, worked hard not to offend her, and asked sincere questions. We were able to develop enough trust in each other that eventually, she allowed our cameras into her home to meet her family and spend the day with them for an interview. Now, you're probably asking yourself, "How did all of this happen in such a short amount of time?" Great question. It boils down to your core values as a reporter.

Renowned entertainment journalist Scott Rover said it better than I can, ""You have to value your relationship with the celebrity more than the dirt of the day." That part.

SCOTT ROVER
ENTERTAINMENT JOURNALIST

EXAMPLE: Octo Mom Signs Reality TV Deal (Us Weekly) * This was all source and back reporting.

WHAT DO EDITORS WANT?

Journalism has evolved from objective reporting to overt sensationalism. Why is this important for you to know?
Put simply; it completely changes the expectations of reporters. Historically, people have relied on traditional
media sources such as newspapers, magazines, radio, and television, but now the majority of people consume
media content via Facebook, TikTok, or YouTube. What this means is that the vast majority of the content you'll
be producing is the digital version of low-hanging fruit. What does this mean? People gravitate towards content
that's attention-grabbing and easily consumable, so, as a reporter, it's important for you to be able to write highly
engaging headlines, captions, and articles that attract audiences from around the world. To achieve this, let's take
a look at some specific things your editors are looking for in modern-day reporters.

1. **Great reporters who understand that social media never sleeps.** Because we have around the-clock
   media, events are often reported within minutes (sometimes even seconds) after they've occurred. Also
   because 'social media never sleeps', there's more competition than ever for clicks, likes, and shares. As
   a result, entertainment newsrooms are chaotic because to be the number one media outlet for celebrity
   journalism; it's a full-fledged race of Who Got There First? For example, news organizations literally hire
   people whose sole job is scouring the internet for illusive celebrity tweets and social media posts that they
   can use for potential stories. Also, tools like Facebook & Instagram Live have allowed celebrity news to
   break at any moment, which means that if your network wants any leverage over the content, it's an all
   hands-on-deck.

2. **Great reporters who understand the nature of competitive celebrity journalism.** Entertainment
   reporters catch a lot of flak for their supposed lack of compassion, especially when tragedy strikes. But
   let's face the facts. This industry is competitive, and if you don't report the story, someone else will. To
   get a handle on this issue, let's examine it from two angles: That of a reporter and that of a celebrity. As
   a reporter, your job is to report the news, whether it's good or bad. This means that sometimes you will
   have to suspend some of your personal beliefs about someone's right to privacy, especially during times of
   personal loss. From the celebrity's point of view, they understand that you have a job to do, and by doing
   it, it brings them fame, money, and attention. However, they are human beings who experience tragedy,
   loss, and sadness like everyone else, which means that when you report the story, their wish is that you
   do so with an element of respect. As such, your editors are looking for you to utilize your impeccable

communication skills to deliver the news in a way that demonstrates compassion for the celebrity without compromising your journalistic duty.

3. **Great reporters who disseminate information quickly.** Because of the constant pressure to share content as soon as possible, great reporters need to be able to publish their stories quickly. This is one of those expectations that evolved from years ago. Before social media, reporters could wait a week to publish a story so that they could fact check, research, and schedule interviews. However, now reporters have to be ready to hop on a Zoom call at a moment's notice to gather the information and publish the story within minutes.

4. **Great reporters who see themselves as an extension of the media, print or magazine brand.** Editors are always looking for great content, so as long as you have stories and ideas that are constantly in motion, your bosses will love you. However, even before you become a reporter, this will make you a stronger reporter because it only takes one story to skyrocket you into editorial fandom. Therefore, developing this mindset early will help you to realize how much is required of you if you want to go from good to great. What this means is that you should always be thinking of yourself as a media company in terms of your social media accounts, website, and content production. For example, start developing your website now rather than later so that people know where they can find and vet you before they hire you to work for their company. In other words, you should be thinking, "My journalism career is going to take off, and, when it does, I want to have everything lined up, ready to go."

CLICKBAIT, ANYONE?

What do you know about headlines, hooks, and leads? When it comes to news consumption, the way people both get their news and how much time they spend reading it has changed. For example, the average attention span on social media is 2 seconds, so you have a much shorter amount of time to get the facts out, which means that even though nearly half of the world's population is on social media, it's getting more difficult to hold people's attention for sustained periods of time. In years past, people would consume longer videos and thoroughly read articles, but this is not the case anymore. In fact, in today's world, there are people whose sole job is to write article titles that grab people's attention. What this means for you is that you need to focus on crafting headlines and hooks that both intrigue and mystify the reader.

Let's look at four key factors that will help you write better hooks, headlines, and leads:

01. Speed.

As an entertainment reporter, you are constantly fighting for time and the press. The newsroom is also chaotic because you're watching events unfold in real-time and how your competitors present the information all within minutes. While years ago, writing articles and interviewing celebrities took time, everything now feels like it's on speed because of technology. This means that not only do you need to be good at writing headlines, but you need to be able to crank them out quickly. How can you improve? First, practice. As you go about your day, whether you think it's dull, boring, or just plain average, start applying headlines to the events happening around you that might invoke your reader's curiosity. While you do it, think of those Tik Tok videos we've all seen where the creators narrate the things happening around them as if they were major life events. As you do this, you'll become a headline-creating machine!

02. Relatability.

News outlets and audiences vary in the entertainment industry. For example, the *National Enquirer* is known to appeal to an older demographic with its extreme and emotionally driven headlines that are (in all honesty) fun to read. Headlines from *Associated Press,* however, appeal to affluent business professionals, so they tend to be more traditional and straightforward. By comparison, *Shaderoom* usually writes controversial, clickbait-driven headlines that evoke a strong emotional reaction on the part of the reader. What's the point of all of this? By studying the different types of headlines and their effects on your target audience, you will become better at writing them, almost as if they were second nature.

03. Teasers.

When celebrities have a big movie coming out, what do they do to promote it? They put out teasers because they stoke the fire of interest, generating excitement and priming audiences for the release date. What I want you to do is take this marketing principle and apply it to your own content. For example, before you're about to release an article, tease your audience by dripping juicy bits of information and engaging followers with teasers like, "It's almost here," "Coming soon," and "Wait for it...". Influencers and celebrities do this with ease because they understand how important it is to garner enthusiasm before releasing some of their core content. Yes, sometimes celebrity reporters indeed have to just get the information out there as quickly as possible, but the best reporters and most successful publications understand that powerful headlines create long-term success and are the difference between people reading your blog, website, or magazine out of hundreds of others. To develop this skill, write at least three to four solid stories, and before you release your content, share teasers that hype up your content.

04. Intrigue.

Your headline's job is to inspire the reader to click the link to your article. However, your article is nothing if no one actually reads it. This is why some subscription-based companies have embraced the "Read More" button. For example, certain websites will provide the reader with the headline and the first paragraph of the article (the lead), but the viewer has to tap the "View More" button to access the rest of the information. This is why the lead-in is critical to your story. To write an awesome lead or hook, focus on the angle of your story and build intrigue around the core information.

MY JOURNEY

Me With Chris Tucker

Interviewing Brankka Katic

Interviewing Ashley Judd

Me With Michael Jai

Me With Jamie Foster Brown

Me With Celo

Me at BET Awards

Interviewing With Omar Mills

Me With Jillian And Bob

Me With Sidney Miller

Me With My Great Friend
Jamiah Adams_ Biz Markie

Interviewing Brian White

Me With Marisa Menunos

Interviewing Lance Gross

Me at M J Funeral

Interviewing Melanie

On The Red Carpet for US Weekly

On The Job

Me Holding the EMMY

Me and Juliette Lewis

Interviewing Christian Bale

Interviewing Naturi Naughton

Public Enemies Premiere

Me at NAACP Awards

Me With Shangela

Me With Oscar Statue

Me With Paula Patton
And Robin Thicke

CHAPTER 3

THE INTERVIEW

LOCATING AND INTERVIEWING SOURCE EXPERTS

The easiest job for a reporter in our technologically advanced world is finding experts to interview. Through a simple social media search, you can connect with experts on everything from childcare, the music industry, to dating. However, as an aspiring reporter you should know that while it's easy to find the experts, the bulk of the work is in the prep work for the interview.

But first, let's talk about how you can find credible experts for your story.

Sometimes your best sources are already in your network. So today, start compiling a list of people that you know and the industries in which they work. For example, are they an authority on technology? A beauty consultant? An expert nutritionist? A pet guru? If so, add them to your network of potential experts.

It's really just as simple as using platforms like LinkedIn and searching for an expert within your particular beat. Additionally, most people you reach out to are more than happy to exchange an interview for free publicity. However, even though it's super rare to receive a rejection to an interview request, you should still prepare yourself because sometimes people are busy and other times there's a scheduling conflict. If that happens, here are some additional platforms to find the perfect source for your interview:

- ➲ **ProfNet –** ProfNet is one of my favorite places to find experts to interview and products to review for potential articles. Simply sign in as a reporter and instantly be connected to hundreds of thousands of experts in a variety of categories and niches. 

- ➲ **Absolute Write –** Absolute Writer is a special community for writers of all levels. There's also a section on the website called The *Absolute Write Water Cooler* that's devoted to interviewing subject requests. 

- ➲ **The ToolBox -** A free resource for start-up newsrooms, legacy and local media, freelancers, entrepreneurs, educators, student media, and people in many other industries. Reporters new to a beat use the pages, organized much like a newsroom, to familiarize themselves with coverage and sourcing. Toolbox content has a Creative Commons license, and educators are encouraged to share Toolbox resources, videos, newsletters, etc. in class and in course materials. (the link for the title of this paragraph is: https://www.journaliststoolbox.org/about/

- ⮂ <u>**Help a Reporter Out**</u> **(HARO) -** This website will be your best friend, but there are some rules that you have to abide by to submit a source request. For example, you cannot backchannel any of the sources and you have to provide a summary of the topic along with your deadline. Also, when you've finished writing your article, you must submit a copy of your final report to the source you quoted.

- ⮂ **Local businesses –** Local businesses are a great source of information for not only lead generation but source experts. If you're looking for specialists, generalists, activists, psychologists, or conservationists they're usually just a phone call away.

- ⮂ **Local Organizations** – There's huge value in partnering with local organizations to get the support you need because every conversation is either an opportunity for a story or a chance to learn something new. For example, when I belonged to a local women's organization, they were always willing to help me out when I needed someone to interview. Also, even if you're just on their email list, you'll stay in the loop by gaining insider knowledge, which only benefits you in the long run.

PREPPING FOR THE INTERVIEW

Think of the top interviews you've listened to on TV or radio. Who was at the helm? Chances are you're thinking of some seriously talented individuals who've earned themselves the right to call themselves household names. While you have them in mind, let's discuss how they conduct themselves so you can prepare for stage two - the interview.

The first thing that separates great reporters from the rest is that they understand the importance of being in alignment with themselves and the person they are interviewing. This means that you're speaking to them as a reporter representing the interests of your network and readers. As such, you have to operate on a higher vibrational level and be above the noise. So how can you achieve this elite interviewing ability?

First, remember that there are two types of languages: vocal and nonverbal. As the interviewer, you want to listen to what someone is saying and watch their body language to look for cues about their feelings, thoughts, and beliefs. For example, how are they moving their hands? Is there any tension in the face, arms, or neck? What's their posture like? Are they making eye contact? Observing these traits enables you to maneuver the interview and spot inconsistencies or holes in their statements so that you can get clarification for your audience. This is what it means to be in alignment with the self, the interviewee, and your readers.

Second, give the person space to talk. While it might be tempting to go straight into the hard-hitting questions, especially in a high-profile interview, it's important to allow the person time to express themselves. Yes, you're still looking out for your audience, but you're also trying to get to know the person and why they came to your platform because the conversation is confirmation. If they're speaking to you, there's a reason why.

Next, to become a successful interviewer, follow these industry gems I've learned:

1. **BE WARM.** The magic behind a great interview is not just in the questions you ask but also in how you make the guest feel. That's why it's important to present a friendly and cooperative demeanor so that your interviewee feels comfortable from the start. As an entertainment reporter, the last thing you want is for your guest feel like they are being interrogated. You want them, to remember you for your warm and inviting tone, whether they're a celebrity or not.

2. **BE EMPATHETIC.** Empathy is the ability to connect and make someone feel seen. Since our world is deeply psychological, the ability to harness the power of mutual understanding is going to take you far in the world of journalism. For example, imagine that you're interviewing a celebrity that has suffered a recent loss. Likely their publicists would tell you that certain questions are off-limits, but you can still

connect by asking, "You've been through a lot these past few years. How have you been able to push through?" You see, rather than directly ask about the tragedy itself, you can allude to their strength in overcoming it, which builds empathy.

3. **BE PREPARED.** While there's no right way to prepare for an interview, it is recommended that you study the individual you're interviewing much like you would for a test in school. Beforehand, you want to research them, listen to old interviews, and take notes on their past answers to important questions.

LISTEN. Additionally, remember to listen to your guest. While it's okay to have notes, it's just as critical to listen to their answers and develop an instinct for when to ask follow-up questions to delve deeper into a topic. To learn this skill, observe other great reporters so you can learn how and when to go off script.

RED CARPET ETIQUETTE

The infamous red carpet always looks shiny and bright but leading up to the moments the bright lights start flashing you want to make sure you can make an impact. Whether that means returning to the newsroom with golden quotes or footage, you want to be on your A-game when it comes to social graces and professional etiquette. But don't let the pressure get to you. In this section, I am going to share with you the top secrets that most reporters rarely get to hear until it's too late.

Ask Important Questions. Years ago, reporters used fashion as an easy segue into Red Carpet interviews with Hollywood's elite. You know the scoop. Usually, they would ask softball questions like, "Who are you wearing?" or "What did you do to get ready for tonight?", but now everything has changed. With campaigns like the #AskHerMore movement, celebrities are looking for reporters to ask more than just superficial questions about the way they look and what they're wearing. That's why it's imperative for you to consider what *they* would like to talk about rather than assuming you know, or worse, winging the interview. For example, perhaps they'd like to discuss a movie script they co-wrote or a film that they starred in and directed. Maybe they have a new pilot project that they want to promote. Perhaps they're pursuing a new business venture. In other words, focus on the inspiration behind their work, and you will position yourself as the knowledgeable and competent professional that you're aspiring to become. *But what about fashion? Aren't the Oscars and Met Gala all about designer clothes and jewelry?* Yes! It's important to blend fashion into your interviews, as there's big money, contractual obligations, and publicity deals behind their outfits, but it's not the *only* topic celebrities want to talk about.

Adapt to Social Changes. A lot has evolved within the social circles of the entertainment industry. For example, today's Hollywood elites are no longer hiding behind the curtain. In fact, most celebrities utilize their social media platforms to promote the causes and organizations they care about the most, which could be great topics for the Red Carpet as long as they're not controversial or confrontational.

Be Social. Not Sloppy. Lastly, there will be lots of alcohol at these events, but the Red Carpet is not the time or the place to lose your wits. While it's okay to have a drink under the right circumstances, keep in mind that most Red-Carpet blunders occur when reporters get a little too loose-lipped and inadvertently put the celebrities on the spot, making them feel uncomfortable. Mistakes like these are costly because we live in a cancel culture world. Simply put, don't do anything that impacts your credibility.

Don't Forget the Original Source. When conducting an interview, you must quote original sources. Why is this important? Aside from the fact that it adds credibility to your reporting, source quoting will protect you from plagiarism, lawsuits, and major fines. Uniquely, in the early 2000s, it was customary for some reporters to use other people's content to present as their own, which created bad blood within the industry and forever blacklisted some celebrity entertainment reporters. However, in today's world, both social media and fact-checking have made it so that each reporter must stand on their own journalistic integrity. This means is that even if you work for a rival network, you still must acknowledge the source of the information you're referencing in your interviews. For example, if you're representing *Us Weekly* on the Red Carpet while interviewing the winner of *People* magazine's *Sexiest Man Alive,* you need to reference the rival magazine when you ask about the award. This is also a branding issue. "Sexiest Man Alive" is associated with *People,* whereas "Person of the Year" is claimed by *Time* magazine which means that if you do not cite them, they will turn to litigation. Always, always, always quote the original source.

Be kind. Bodies change as we age. We may gain weight, have a breakout, or experience hormonal shifts. All of these are a normal part of human bodily functions, but Hollywood takes criticism to another level. Celebrities are constantly scrutinized for how they look to the point that even going to the gym or local coffee shop without full hair and makeup is met with a barrage of questions and accusations about their mental health or emotional stability. Thankfully, though, numerous A-listers have clapped back on all forms of body shaming, highlighting their struggles with self-esteem and various eating disorders. For you as a reporter, honor these changes and recognize that any comments or questions on a celebrity's physical evolution are unwelcome at best. Yes, use discretion even when asking them about the changes they had to undergo to play a movie role. For example, instead of saying, *"You had to lose a lot of weight to play this role. Tell us what that was like,"* say, *"We all witnessed your incredible transformation for this role. Is there anything you'd like to share regarding your experiences as you underwent that process?"* In other words, reference their efforts in your interviews, not their bodies. If you do, you will gain their respect as an advocate for body positivity.

The red carpet is yours. Own it.

CHAPTER 4

THE INSIDER SCOOP

A DAY IN THE LIFE OF A CELEBRITY REPORTER

It's all in the details. During award shows, when I would gather observations, many times, these items would lead to stories. New relationships, a baby on the way, new ventures and so on! So, keep your eyes open whenever you are at an event.

Oftentimes you will gather reports from on the-record transcriptions, speeches, statements, or news conferences. Also, you may have to go to the courthouse, reach out to a publicist, or even verify the information. So, the source is just the tip of the iceberg. There's much more to every story.

From covering breaking news to researching features, reporter have a lot of variety in their day-to-day work. If you're thinking of becoming a reporter, you might be wondering what a day in the life of a reporter looks like. Are you likely to spend most of your time writing, or will you be conducting a lot of interviews? The answer will depend on your specific role, but most journalists do a combination of the following things:

Staying on top of news trends

Since journalism is all about what's happening at the moment, one of the key parts of any journalist's day is to stay on top of news trends by checking newswires, news magazines, popular blogs, and social media platforms such as Twitter and Facebook. Doing this throughout the day allows journalists to come up with an editorial plan and assign reporters to stories that need to be covered.

Researching stories

Once a reporter has their assignment, they're responsible for conducting in-depth research into the story. This includes identifying potential sources, fact checking numbers, dates and other important pieces of information and doing contextual research to find out related news items that should be referenced in the final piece.

A day in the life of a celebrity reporter

Interviewing people

Another important part of a journalist's day is to go out and interview people. This can include talking to voters outside of a polling station when covering an election, interviewing medical experts about a new advancement in medicine or chatting with a celebrity about their latest film. Whatever the context of the story, journalists are responsible for getting the information straight from the source and then synthesizing this information into a story that they can share with the public.

Writing and editing

After researching the story and conducting interviews, journalists spend time identifying the key points of the story and creating a structure for it. They then use the information they've gathered to add detail and color to the story and to make it as informative as possible before sending it to an editor for review and publication.

An exciting and challenging career path, journalism offers recent grads the opportunity to be at the frontline of breaking news while also helping them develop engaging storytelling skills. To find out if being a reporter is right for you, consider doing an internship with a news or media outlet.

PROTECT YOURSELF

Picture it. Hollywood. The early 2000s.

You're living your best life as a news reporter, and you're good at what you do. You take great photos, your interview skills are on point, and you're great with people.

Then, you unearth a bombshell of a story - the type that catapults reporters to journalism superstardom. However, you have no idea what this story could mean for your career, so you do what any new reporter would do. You go straight to your editors with adrenaline pumping through your veins and share the scoop with your bosses. They congratulate you on this huge break, and you leave the meeting with a glow.

You can't wait to see how this story develops. You also speak with the individuals with whom you're writing the story about, and they personally request that you fly out to conduct the interview.

You're going to be an integral part of not just the team but the creative process. All is right with the world, right?

Wrong.

Unbeknownst to you, the arrangements are made for the interview team to fly out and get the story without you. On top of that, the article is published without any acknowledgement of your work to break the story.

The story of a lifetime was just robbed right before your eyes by the very people you thought you could trust.

This is all too common in the entertainment industry. Due to the sheer amount of competition and the speed at which news is delivered, something like this could happen to you as it did to me. With that, I want to give you some of my top tips for protecting yourself as a professional reporter.

RULE #1: PUT EVERYTHING IN WRITING

Before disclosing any information about the story, I told my team that I should have made sure that I would either receive credit for the work in the publication or be a part of the team that conducted the interviews in writing. And, honestly, it's as simple as having a conversation with your bosses. For example, you could say, *"I want to thank you for the opportunity to be a part of your team, and I believe that my efforts have paid off. There's an important story that I just unearthed, and before it's revealed, I want to make sure I'm going to receive the proper acknowledgements specified in the email I sent you.* For me, having a conversation like this could have changed everything, but because I was new and excited, I was easily iced out of the equation. The lesson here is to ensure you have everything in writing to protect your sources, your content, and, most importantly, yourself.

Rule #2: Protect Your Sources

In today's world, journalism would be dead without anonymous source reporting. Retaliation is a threat for the whistleblowers and informants that we rely on as journalists, which is why it's critical that you protect the identities of your sources. Additionally, anonymity in source reporting holds people accountable because if no one could ever report the truth without fear of retribution, then there would be no transparency in society. Also, remember that in celebrity journalism, people are becoming more suspicious of your intent while reporting or writing a story. Celebrities constantly reference the media, and how they will take their words out of context and twist them to tell a story that does not accurately reflect what happened. You've likely witnessed celebrity feuds - both real and produced - where the media has made a situation seem far bigger than it is. So, as you move up the ladder in celebrity journalism, stay genuine and treat your sources with respect. If you do, they will return the favor a million times over.

Rule #3: Stay Within The Boundaries

One of the ways to cultivate trust with your sources is to stay within the boundaries of what's been said during an interview. For example, you will want to record the interview and then have it transcribed. The app Otter.ai is great for this because it records and transcribes simultaneously. Then, as you write the story, you can quote verbatim what the individual said. Now, as a professional writer, you do have some liberty to edit the quote for errors and overall comprehensibility, but do not alter the essence of what was said. Lastly, maintain an organized file of all of these records so that you have documentation that upholds what you wrote in case of a complaint.

Rule #4: Know Your Rights[2]

Whether you're building your online presence, or you've just got hired at a major celebrity news outlet, you want to know the company's expectations along with any rights you may have as you cover sensitive material. Additionally, based on your location, your rights as a journalist vs. the rights of celebrities vary from state to state. To start, a good habit to get into is getting written consent from the person you're interviewing or writing about before you publish your story. Additionally, your editors are going to push you to get the story at all costs. Celebrity journalism has become quite aggressive in terms of what's publicized, but keep in mind that no matter how much pressure you may feel to get to the scoop, your relationship with the celebrity matters more in the long run. Also, as demand for your content increases, you are likely to start to develop business relationships with others that require a contract. Make sure that you've read the contract completely and that you understand *everything* in it. If something is not to your liking, ask questions. Under no circumstances should you sign an agreement blindly. Lastly, to bone up on your legal knowledge, you may want to grab a copy of the book *Law for Journalists.*

Rule #5: Protect Your Content

As you build your online presence, you will want to protect your content from copyright infringement. Typically, you don't have to worry about major news outlets stealing your content, but smaller companies and creators may aim to present your photos, videos, and articles as their own. That's why it's vital for you to make sure that your blog is legally protected. To do this, you will want to consult a lawyer to obtain a) a privacy policy, b) a terms and conditions page, and c) a disclaimer. These are documents that outline user permissions and expectations for both you and the consumer that form a legally binding agreement between you/your company, and your readers.

Second, when you start producing more newsworthy content, larger companies are likely to reach out to you either for higher or to ask for your consent to share your information. This is fantastic because it validates your talent; however, many new reporters to the industry get taken advantage of because they either don't understand the agreement they're signing, or they have trouble in the negotiation process to obtain fair compensation. The first step to doing business in this industry is to read the entire contract and make sure that you understand exactly what's expected of you and the company as well as what both parties are entitled to according to the agreement.

---

2   *The information provided in this book does not, and is not intended to, constitute legal advice; instead, all information, content, and materials available herein are for general informational purposes only. Information may not constitute the most up-to-date legal or other information, so please consult a lawyer to learn more about your rights.*

Do not sign any documents until you know exactly what you're agreeing to. The second rule of business is to remember that if an organization is reaching out to you, they *want* your content. This means that you should never settle for the first offer. Learn to negotiate the deal, which may take some practice and mindset work on your part, to get the highest value for your content because you're absolutely worthy of fair compensation. Afterall, they contacted YOU.

Now, how do you know how much is a fair price for your piece of content? This is where your research skills as a reporter will come in handy. Find out what the going rate is for a story or a photo. Once you have this information, you will know when someone actually values your work or is just trying to low-ball you. Also, you should always be thinking of yourself as a media agency, not just a reporter. Why? First, this shows that you value what you do, and when companies see that you're able to put together a good story that's been verified or fact-checked consistently, they will, too. Second, when you view your life as an extension of your personal brand as a reporter, you'll view the world through a different lens. You'll start instinctually identifying leads and potential content for huge stories, and that's a pretty lucrative position to be in.

To conclude, good reporters understand that entertainment journalism is a complex industry that captivates audiences, shapes the fabric of our culture, and connects the lifeblood of Hollywood superstardom to our daily lives. This industry is also considered multimedia journalism, which means that each story that you write is unique and can take on a life of its own based on the way it's presented to the world. For example, in today's fast-paced world, you want to put out not just written content but also that which enhances your story with videos, images, and interviews to add credibility and flair that will forever marinate in the minds of your readers. To do this, always consider the best way to utilize your sources and resources in an ethical and legal manner, both digitally and in print media.

RESUME REVIEW

To land an entry-level job in the entertainment industry, there are five* key qualifiers your resume should contain before you apply:

1. **A mission statement.** At the top of your resume should be a mission statement that aligns with the company's goals of producing top-level content to enhance the consumer experience. The purpose of this is to show that you're not an average job seeker; you're actively aligning your skills for a common purpose.

> **SAMPLE MISSION STATEMENT:**
>
> Accomplished and self-motivated entertainment reporter seeking a creative role at an award-winning celebrity news organization. Possesses a robust talent for diverse and dynamic storytelling along with the skills to cultivate long-lasting sources for the publisher on a wide variety of beats.

2. **A body of work.** Attached to your resume, you will want to provide at least 3 clips that demonstrate your skills across a variety of niches and topics. Your copy should be clean, accurate, error-free, and publish-ready. The big takeaway here is not to limit yourself to your resume in this field. Industry leaders want to verify your skills as well as see how you approach the job to get results.

3. **Links to your social media.** One of the best ways to showcase your work and how you engage audiences is to provide links to your social media pages. The industry leaders are going to look at them anyway, but it demonstrates confidence if you provide them yourself as well as have them ready for prime-time analysis. Here you will want to show your skills and versatility in terms of content production (i.e., videos, reels, blogs, lives, stories, and/or posts) related to your niche. This helps people to identify who you are and what you do without putting in guesswork.

4. **Include a cover letter.** Your cover letter is usually the first impression the company will have of you, so it should be customized to each job you're applying for, as well as highlight your level of experience and qualifications that make you an excellent candidate. To do this, start your letter by addressing the hiring manager. (Do not use words such as "Hello", "Hey", or "Hi" to begin your cover letter.) If you do not know specifically whom you're writing to, you can always write *Dear [Insert Manager's Job Title]* or the name of

the department. Second, reference the job that you're applying for in the first paragraph. *Please accept this cover letter and attached resume as my interest in the x-position.* In the next paragraph, highlight your current duties and responsibilities and the areas in which you excel the most. In the following paragraph, discuss how your current role has allowed you to grow professionally and what the payoff has led to in terms of your ability to get results. In your concluding paragraph, you can discuss one personal area of interest or hobby to give your resume a human element and then highlight the attributes that you possess that make you the right fit for this company. Finally, thank the individual for their consideration and express your interest in further communication.

5. **A Digital Portfolio.** In today's competitive world, hiring managers are looking for more than just talented individuals. They're also looking for people who fit within their company's culture. So, when it comes to your cover letter and resume you will want to send them in a visually appealing PDF format that provides a link to your website that houses your portfolio. With regards to your website, easy navigation is key, as this makes the publishers want to learn more about you. Your website should also be eye-catching, contain samples of your work, and tell your personal story. Remember, your website is your brand, and the faster people can learn more about you, the easier it is for them to make the decision to hire you.

STORIES FROM THE RED CARPET

RIHANNA – BLOG WRITING

Rihanna: I Can't Stop Losing Weight

LEANN RIMES – BACKREPORTING

was tasked to go back to report on the bar that Leann Rimes was at. It was shared that someone saw her there, and I ended up being the first person to see the infamous video. Watch it here.

Married LeAnn Rimes Having Steamy
Affair with Sexy Costar (US WEEKLY)

BRISTOL PALIN AND LEVI JOHNSTON ENGAGEMENT – SOURCE REPORTING

This cover story was my huge exclusive during my time at US Weekly. I brought the source to the magazine that wanted to give us the story. I got a byline for this story and also a personal letter from Jan Wenner, the man himself.

Bristol Palin, Levi Johnston
Are Engaged! (US Weekly)

Letter from Jann Wenner

SEAN PENN AND SCARLETT JOHANNSEN – FIELD REPORTING

I worked on the Reese Witherspoon wedding weekend in Ojai! This alone deserves its own chapter. The way my colleague and I swooned and laughed so hard that weekend. We ended up in the spa with Reese and her mother and at the restaurant, where we had a front seat to Sean Penn and Scarlett having a full on make-out session. I was the best! Talk about not blowing your cover!!!

Online: Scarlett Johansson, Sean Penn
Debut Romance at Reese's Wedding

DAVID CARRADINE – FAMILY/FRIENDS OUTREACH

One of the hardest things for me as a journalist is reaching out to family members when there is a death in the family. Fortunately, the David Carradine brothers were open and willing to talk to me. A great interview and was posted online completely. WHICH RARELY HAPPENS.

Brother: David Carradine Was the
"Greatest Maverick" (US WEEKLY)

LANCE ARMSTRONG – SOCIAL MEDIA SCOOP

Pretty simple reporting. Since the internet makes it so hard sometimes to get exclusive reporting, and with Twitter, celebs often make announcements themselves. However, magazines pride themselves on being the first to report it. I just happened to be signed onto Twitter and saw that Lance made the announcement of his new arrival. Alerted my editors and Wahla!

RIHANNA – SOURCE REPORTING

FANTASIA – COVER STORY

This was one of my first cover stories, and after many attempts of coordinating to get Fantasia on the telephone before the deadline, it didn't happen. So, I had to improvise and use the quotes that I had and also research to get the cover story together on time!!!!! I did it, and it went well.

LAILA ALI – STORY PITCH

I pitched the idea for US MAGAZINE to do a baby blog with Laila, and she's NOW doing it! Thanks for coming aboard, Laila!

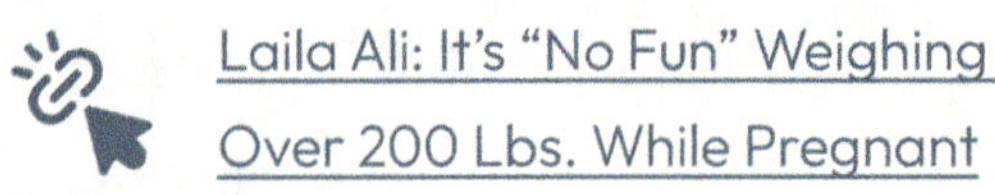
Laila Ali: It's "No Fun" Weighing Over 200 Lbs. While Pregnant

Tia Mowry - Exclusive Interview

As I became more seasoned as a senior reporter, I did more scheduled shoots and less field work. During this interview with Tia Mowry, we met cutie pie Cree, her son. I oversaw the photo shoot and did the interview.

AT HOME INTERVIEW: Exclusive: Meet Tia Mowry's Baby Son Cree!

KOFI SIRIBOE – INTERVIEW

'Straight Outta Compton' Actor Kofi Siriboe on Capturing the Era of NWA (EURWEB.COM)

CHRIS TUCKER & FRIENDS /LEON SULLIVAN FOUNDATION – EVENT COVERAGE

This event coverage resulted in me going to Tanzania, Africa, with Chris Tucker and friends! It was a magical time.

 EVENT COVERAGE: Leon Sullivan Summit
Hosted by Chris Tucker (BRE MAGAZINE)

ABOUT THE AUTHOR

Tanisha Quilter-Williams brings a unique worldview shaped by a colorful background. From growing up as a "military brat," to working in the trenches at some of Hollywood's top companies. Working at ICM, WMA, Inside Edition, E! Entertainment, and US Weekly introduced her to experiences that landed her on the red-carpet interviewing celebrities, such as, Oprah Winfrey, Catherine Zeta-Jones, Denzel Washington, and Kelsey Grammar. During her time at US Weekly, she played a major part in bringing one of the biggest cover stories to US Weekly Magazine when she negotiated the Levi Johnston and Bristol Palin engagement cover story. In 2013, Tanisha left the journalism world behind to pursue her passion for screenwriting. However, years later, she felt that the experience she gained as a journalist could help others, and she decided to write "Got Scoop," Tips on Working as a Celebrity Reporter to help others hone their craft.

Now, Tanisha works in real estate, and after going back to school to obtain her MFA in Creative Writing, she hasn't looked back. To date, she has written and produced a fiction podcast drama called "Forties AF," about three forty-something single friends who pick up the pieces their thirties left behind. Forties AF is in its second season and has been downloaded 100,000 times to date. The audience is growing, and we are seeking funding to turn it into a web series. The podcast was chosen to participate in Gotham Pitch Week 2021 and was nominated as BEST FICTION PODCAST by the Podcast Awards-People's Choice to be announced on September 30, 2021. Tanisha has also just finished writing and producing a dramatic short film called JAMES, about a mother who comes to grips with her young daughter's secret and working on a thriller project called "Prayer Request."

Tanisha is a graduate of California State-University - Los Angeles. Class of 2017